131 WAYS

TO WIN WITH ACCOUNTABILITY

Best Practices for
Driving *Better Results*

HENRY J. EVANS

Author of *Winning with Accountability*

&

ELAINE BIECH

Inquiries regarding permission for use of the material contained in this book should be addressed to:
CornerStone Leadership Institute

P.O. Box 764087
Dallas, TX 75376
972.298.8377

Printed Worldwide
First Printing 2026
First Edition 2026

ISBN: 978-0-9961469-6-8

10 9 8 7 6 5 4 3 2 1

Interior Book Design by Walt's Book Design
www.waltsbookdesign.com

Copy Editor Kathleen Green,
Positively Proofed, Plano, TX,
info@positivelyproofed.com

For my father, Carl Evans

Who always held me accountable; with love, compassion, and kindness.

Who modeled what humility and self-development look like in action. A lifetime learner, father, and friend.

I love you and miss you.

– Henry J. Evans

CONTENTS

INTRODUCTION

Imagine if . . .

- you could count on every person on your team to hit every reasonable deadline;
- your team worked together to proactively prevent surprises and frustrations;
- your organization became the industry leader at implementing innovative strategies, outperforming competitors at every turn;
- you had complete confidence that every person in your organization was willing and able to make changes to help them win in business and in life; and,
- your team enthusiastically looked forward to work every day.

I f all of these imagined goals became reality, would life and work be easier and more enjoyable? Of course. Most people on your team want to be successful. They need to know what to do, and *you* can help them. Are you willing to pay the price required for your team to win? If you are, we encourage you to take a risk and teach your team how to win, starting with how you model accountability.

Several years ago, Henry was backstage warming up for his first public match as a competitive martial artist. He was excited and nervous, and he could hear the crowd cheering for his opponent. It was loud and intimidating. Feeling scared, Henry told his coach he was afraid to lose and look foolish in front of all those people.

Perhaps you have experienced that awful feeling— the fear of losing. It is a gut-wrenching, horrific feeling. Henry's coach understood the anxiety—he had probably faced it before. He put his hand on Henry's shoulder, looked him in the eyes, and offered comfort and wisdom, "Henry, if you don't believe you're going to win, please don't compete. I'll support you either way."

The coach conveyed that the most significant part of winning is to begin with a positive mindset. That lesson— believing that you can win—is critical in all you do.

This book is written to encourage you to lead others to win. It will help you become a positive agent of change for your organization, and help you lead others to win, regardless of their formal title or position. As the coach taught Henry, if you are going to play, play to win.

If you have read our best-selling business book, *Winning with Accountability—The Secret Language of High-Performing Organizations*, participated in our award-winning eSchool, or have attended our classes, you'll be familiar with some of these concepts. We have taken these concepts and broken them down into easy, actionable tips—131 of them—to help you achieve greater results in your organization.

Although much has changed since *Winning with Accountability* was published, most issues in the workplace are the same. Gallup's 2017 "State of America Workplace Report"1 found that only about one-third of America's workers are engaged with their organization's purpose and priorities. Fifty-one percent are not engaged and 16 percent are actively disengaged.

---

1 Gallup State of the American Workplace Report 2017. Retrieved at https://news. gallup.com/reports/199961/state-american-workplace-report-2017.aspx

Deadlines are still missed, expectations are not clear, responsibilities are not identified, and roles are unclear. The problems are the same, even though we have better technology and more efficient platforms. We still experience unclear expectations and broken promises. Relying on technology to fix human mistakes is the same as an amateur automobile driver relying on a standard, off-the-line sports car to make him a world-class Formula One racer. It's not going to happen!

Your team can do better if they know what to do. For sustained success, your team has to get the basics right. This book will help you do just that. Inside these pages are 131 tools and ideas based on our clients' collective wisdom. If your team implements even a portion of these tips, your organization will become more accountable, more successful, and more enjoyable to lead. In short, you can learn to master accountability with simple ideas and actions. Believe that you can impact your organization's culture and results. Our clients do, and so can you.

131 Ways to Win with Accountability can become your team's new language. Every tip is designed to translate language into action. If you moved to another country, your transition would be easier if you learned the native language. Through our 131 tips, we are giving you the language to survive and even thrive in the business world. We've studied and worked with the highest-performing people and organizations. These tips represent their *secret language and successful actions*. The easiest way to learn that new language is to jump right into your team's accountability journey.

By applying our accountability ways, you can take your organization on the path to accelerating performance, strengthening culture, and gaining a competitive advantage. This book is meant as an overview, not an all-encompassing reference. Whether you are in a leadership position or not, you can implement the tips immediately to increase your effectiveness.

What will you achieve? By learning and using the Language of Accountability,™ you will:

- Be more productive and effective;
- Make realistic commitments and meet your deadlines;
- Practice tips to schedule your time more effectively;
- Gain confidence and your colleagues' respect; and,
- Help lead your organization's change, no matter where you sit on the org chart.

Here's how you can get the most out of this book:

- Be ready to highlight the book's pages. Mark keywords or phrases that pertain to your personal situation.
- Read all the way through once then read a chapter a day for the next eight days.
- Educate others about *131 Ways*.

Read, enjoy, and apply the *131 Ways to Win with Accountability* that work for you.

CHAPTER 1

ACCOUNTABILITY LANGUAGE IS THE PATH TO RESULTS

Kelly stared at the rain pouring on her windshield, not sure if she could handle driving.

How did it get to this point? She had finally found her ideal job only 4 miles from home. She liked her boss and her coworkers. She thought she was doing what was expected of her. Yet, she was terminated just a week before finishing her probationary period. They cited a "lack of fit with the culture," as the HR specialist stated. Kelly didn't see it coming.

She tried to think back to the beginning—the very first day. Juan, her boss, gave her an enthusiastic welcome, introduced her to the team, and immediately assigned her something she'd done on previous jobs: designing a leadership development plan. He'd said it was critical and that the top brass wanted to see it ASAP. Feeling the urgency, she'd immediately scheduled meetings with executives to determine organizational needs. In hindsight, she realized she should have asked more questions.

When Juan asked for the plan three weeks later, he was visibly disappointed when she shared the initial results of her interviews. He was expecting a schedule of events, a budget, and the return on investment. When she tried to apologize, saying that her interpretation of the assignment was different, Juan cut her off in mid-sentence. Nodding his head as she explained that it would take more time, Juan assigned two other staff members to help because they had plenty of time.

Even though he was obviously frustrated that she would need at least another month to identify expectations, resources, and existing technology, he told her to take until the end of the month. Four weeks were doable. Unfortunately, the two assigned staffers had few skills in talent development. The reason they had "lots of time" was because they were experts at avoiding work. Since they'd been in the department for a long time, Kelly didn't feel comfortable sharing this with Juan. In fact, she noticed that the culture was not conducive to upward feedback.

When Juan asked for the plan the morning of the 21st, Kelly said she thought she had 10 more days before "the end of the month." That afternoon, HR requested to see her. And now here she was—dismissed.

What could she have done differently? What had she learned? She pulled out her journal and made a few notes.

Culture: It must ensure everyone is personally accountable for all actions, including keeping superiors informed and asking for more information when they aren't specific. This is especially true in a fast-paced environment.

Language: The words used must ensure everyone understands them clearly and in the same way. ASAP, end of the month, or even "a plan" mean different things to different people.

Expectations: Expectations must be clearly defined. It was clear that she and Juan had different ideas about the desired outcome of the "leadership development plan." In addition, she could have checked in more often, using milestones instead of a final due date.

Ability: She had the ability to succeed, yet the support assigned to her did not. She didn't just need more "time." She needed to clearly define the skills of those who could help her.

Rewards and consequences: These must be clearly spelled out for successes and failures. She had no idea Juan was disappointed enough to let her go.

Kelly had an a-ha moment, recognizing that the responsibility was as much hers as it was Juan's. She realized the entire situation was about accountability, and accountability was all about being clear. Looking at the lessons she learned, she realized that the first letter of each of her notes spelled "clear." "Well," she thought, "I should be able to remember that next time!"

Accountability: What's the big deal? You either do it or you don't.

Well, it *is* a big deal. Accountability ensures that the organization achieves its goals—faster and better than competitors. It strengthens team collaboration and performance and promotes individual ownership by aligning employees to the business strategy. These advantages are reason enough for all leaders to focus on accountability, right? Unfortunately, no.

Based on our experience, only about half of employees in organizations are held accountable. Although accountability is viewed as important, achieving it is elusive. Some believe accountability only counts when things go wrong. Clear goals are critical. Yet our research with more than 3,500 executives and managers shows that only 9 percent are very clear about outcomes and only 6 percent say that projects meet expectations.2

So what gives? Why would such a valuable skill be so blatantly ignored? We believe that accountability is intellectually simple but behaviorally complex.

The ideas are easy to understand, but it's difficult to change behaviors and implement the concepts. It requires action and practice.

---

2 Dynamic Results' study of 3,500 leaders in more than 900 organizations over eight years.

Tips for Clear Accountable Language

1. **Make it visual.** No matter what outcome you are working to create, make sure everyone involved has the same mental "picture" of the desired end state. For example, instead of saying, "Let's publish a report," say, "Let's publish a three-slide PowerPoint deck, with an image of a map taking up half of the space of each slide."

2. **Specificity isn't always clear.** Have you ever been in the middle of a conversation and found that you and the other person are talking about two different things? That's because the meanings of words are in people's minds, not dictionaries. People have their own meanings for words like "plan" or "best." Be as specific as you can be, and always check to see if you are being *specific enough*.

3. **Sound the alert.** If you are like most employees, you've seen the same problem occur again and again, but no one ever sounds the alarm. Be the voice your organization needs. Be willing to proclaim that something needs to change to increase accountability.

4. **Schedule realistic due dates.** Do you get stressed over unrealistic deadlines? Do your part to keep

time and dates realistic. There is no need to create stress by inflicting self-imposed, unreasonable time and date requirements.

5. **Work in the zone.** We mean the time zone. Clarity is assured when a date, time, and time zone are included in all commitments. Use it with your clients, customers, and colleagues. Adding a simple CDT (Central Daylight Time), or whatever time zone you are referring to, is a good habit.

6. **Share the CLEAR list.** Your life will be easier when everyone understands the five requirements for establishing accountability. It can serve as a reminder to be more clear. (No pun intended.)

    *   Culture: How I inspire and encourage communication with others
    *   Language: What I say to generate shared understanding
    *   Expectations: How I describe the results
    *   Ability: How I ensure the skills, knowledge, and resources are available
    *   Reward and consequences: What we will gain or risk

7. **Choose the best project owner.** How do you determine the best owner? The most technically qualified person may not always be the best person for

ownership. Typically the best owner has great project management skills and is enthusiastic about the project. An enthusiastic person who is less qualified may work harder and be more successful, especially at inspiring others to do their personal best.

8. **Owners must manage.** Make your projects more successful by selecting project owners who have management skills, such as establishing timelines, delegating, and communicating the end result. Management skills are a basic necessity.

9. **Owners must own.** You can save yourself time when you allow the owner to own the action. Do not interfere with the owner's process. Direct anyone who has questions or suggestions to take them directly to the owner. As a requester, establish "what" (we are accomplishing). Allow the owner to name "how" (we will do it).

10. **Know their limitations.** How can you ensure that others will be successful? Learn what people are capable of and don't task them with more. If a team lacks capacity or resources, adjust quickly. Invite them to reevaluate what they are trying to accomplish, and work toward results that are achievable. Asking an employee to accomplish something they

are not capable of is leadership failure, not employee failure.

11. **Measurement's a must.** If you can't measure it, don't ask for it. Quantify exactly what you want to happen and avoid unmeasurable words like "better." What specifically makes it better? If someone left before work started and returned upon completion, what would they see that was different (more inventory, fewer accidents, 2 percent increase in associate engagement)?

12. **No questions unanswered.** How can you be sure you are clear? Clear expectations mean that enough communication occurs so that no questions are unanswered at the end of every interaction. Ask your questions—all of them—and make space for others to do the same!

13. **Give the gift of clarity.** Even when you think you've been clear, ask listeners what they heard. Feedback informs you of how your message was received. People act on what they heard, not on what you think you said.

14. **Identify what's lacking.** Is your team running as smoothly as you'd like? No? Determine the reasons and if some are related to a lack of accountability, such as changing (or conflicting) priorities, unclear

expectations, a lack of ownership, absence of consequences, unclear roles or responsibilities, lack of collaboration, or lack of transparency. Create a list to
help you understand what you might do. Go ahead!
You've got ideas.

CHAPTER 2

THE ACCOUNTABILITY JOURNEY STARTS WITH YOU

Minnette just left her supervisor's office with a request to locate a coach for the new VP of accounting by next week. What was he thinking, assigning her another task with an impossible deadline?! She wonders, "Did he forget about the PR campaign for the new store opening? What about the community fundraising golf tournament he asked her to coordinate? Tomorrow is the deadline for the Journal article." Minnette knows that finding a coach will go on the back burner.

The boss doesn't pay her enough to be a miracle worker!

Minnette's supervisor may have been out of touch with reality, but Minnette was responsible, too. She should have clarified what was possible. A culture of accountability exists when team members hold themselves and each other accountable in a positive and productive manner. To make this happen, these four requirements must be embedded in every request:

- *Clarity*—creates a picture so that there is no question about what completion looks like.
- *Specific date, time, and time zone*—especially if your organization has offices in several countries or you interact with others in multiple time zones.
- *Ownership*—specifies only one person owns the task.
- *Sharing*—telling someone about a commitment to ensure accountability.

Accountability starts with you. When you believe (truly believe) that you help build an accountable culture, you are off to a good start on your journey.

Tips for Your Successful Journey

15. **Set high expectations for yourself.** To make a difference, set your sights high. Others will take notice of your stretch goals and join in. Inspired colleagues will set their own targets higher, and the momentum will multiply. Be "stretchy," not "breaky." Challenge people to stretch to achieve greater results, but don't push them to the breaking point.

16. **Begin positively.** Having doubts? Believe, without hesitation, that you can make a positive difference. You have the power to model a winning mindset. Begin with your own attitude, regardless of your title. Know without a doubt that you contribute to your organization's success.

17. **Accountability is a two-way street.** If you accepted a task that was not specific and clear, you are still responsible if it fails. Always ask for clarity and specificity before accepting and agreeing to a new assignment. What will the final product look like? When is it due—date, time, and time zone? It takes two to dance the accountability tango; everyone needs to listen to the same band.

18. **Schedule it.** Only make commitments that you are certain you have the time to complete. In fact, it's

best to block time on your calendar for each commitment. Even better—don't commit without a calendar in hand.

19. **Can't do what you can't see.** Are you confused about objectives? When writing objectives, use words that can be seen. You can't see *improved* or *good*. Use words that can be counted or seen or touched, such as "50 percent more," "63 sets," or "full-color copies." Less specific: "Improve performance." More specific: "Achieve sales of $1.3 million."

20. **Only one owner.** Assign ownership of any measurable outcome to one person. Even if part of the task has been delegated to others, the owner is the one person accountable for the results. Don't be tempted to assign a task to a team, department, or group. It's a recipe for failure. To whom do we bring changes?

21. **Make it your mantra.** Use this mantra to help you easily remember the four parts of an accountability request: "Who will do what by when, and who needs to be informed about this?"

22. **End only when the assignment is complete.** How do you know when an assignment is complete? Whether you're giving or receiving a commitment,

ensure that all four requirements—clarity, specificity, ownership, and sharing—are embedded in the request before the interaction has ended.

23. **Step up to the plate.** You, too, can become an accountability superhero! When you see something that needs to be done, step up and take it on. Become the owner. Find a project that needs to be addressed. Then accept personal responsibility for tackling it. Every situation can be improved with a mindset of passion, determination, and perseverance. Ask, "What else can I do?"

24. **Go beyond your job expectations.** Don't let your job description hold you back. Go above and beyond whenever you can. Demonstrate a learner's mindset, (i.e., a desire to learn continuously by asking to be trained in something new).

25. **Ask others to hold you accountable.** Are you looking for a way to improve? For example, if you recognize and want to stop cutting others off in mid-sentence, ask your team to call you on it.

26. **Ask your boss before it happens.** Have you ever had that sinking feeling when you didn't know how to do something? Prepare by asking your boss, "How should I communicate with you when I don't know how to do something or if I need support?" Better

to cover all possibilities before something comes crashing down!

27. **Prevent *voluntold* volatility.** You missed a meeting and were assigned a task! Isn't that infuriating? Establish a procedure for addressing *voluntold* situations (when you are given an assignment but were not present). Include who has the right to voluntell whom, what type of work is appropriate, how to adjudicate issues, and what questions need to be asked before assigning tasks.

28. **Eradicate excuses.** Identify your favorite excuse. It could be "I didn't know how," or "I didn't have time," or some other reason for why you didn't do what you agreed to do. Replace your excuses with two clear steps: Own it and offer a call to action— "You are right. I didn't make it a priority. Here's when I will get it to you."

29. **Intuition is your friend.** Intuition is a good predictor of future success or failure. Don't make a commitment that you know in your heart you are not likely to meet.

30. **Know when to say "no."** Have you been asked to do something and know you won't be able to succeed? Find a comfortable way to say, "No, I can't do that." In the long run, people will respect you more

for saying "no" than they will if you give a false "yes" and fail to deliver. Not comfortable saying "no?" Try "not right now."

31. **Actions above excuses.** Demonstrate that your actions rise above your excuses. Accept responsibility when things go wrong, and own your mistakes. Then demonstrate what you'll do to rectify the situation. Being transparent and vulnerable ensures respect and demonstrates accountability.

CHAPTER 3

DRIVE ACCOUNTABILITY INTO THE CULTURE

Have you ever wondered why people think "accountability" is a bad word? Actually, there are some pretty good reasons. The most common is that accountability is usually associated with *blame* after something has gone wrong. In addition, responsibilities are expanded or overlap, priorities change midway, everyone is rewarded whether results were met or not, and consequences are diluted or seldom occur. These inconsistencies prevent employees from seeing the connection between results and rewards. This may lead to resentment by those who are perceived to work harder or contribute more. All of these become roadblocks to a culture of accountability.

No wonder the word "accountability" sends chills up people's spines. Fortunately, there is something that you can do to make accountability a positive word and a part of your organizational culture.

Tips to Create an Accountable Culture

32. **A culture of accountability takes time and patience.** What's your role in an accountable culture? It begins with clear goals for the organization. You can help ensure that everyone—from the bottom to the top—is working toward the same goals and holding each other accountable.

33. **Lead accountability.** You can lead accountability— yes, YOU—no matter your job title or place on the organizational chart. You can help develop an accountable culture by demonstrating integrity and transparency, following through on commitments, communicating clearly, and making others feel safe to express their thoughts. How would you rate yourself on these?

34. **Hire people with proven accountability.** Is there an easier way to spread a future of accountability? Start by hiring the right people. Ask probing questions that show how the potential hires dealt with past situations. For example, you could ask how the person did the right thing or honored a commitment even though the action created personal hardship. Probe for details. Does the candidate blame others, make

excuses, focus on the problems or accept responsibility with a focus on solutions?

35. **Introduce accountability on day 1.** Accountability starts with onboarding. Ensure that new employees understand the culture of accountability, the language of accountability, and what this means for their jobs. Pair them up with those who can share examples and expectations over the first couple of months as they become a part of the workforce.

36. **Use inclusive words.** How can you show you're all in? You can embed accountability into the culture by changing the way you discuss tasks. For example, include yourself by saying, "we are accountable for …" or "we can meet this deadline."

37. **Share with others.** When we share a commitment with others in an accountable culture, we are automatically asking them to hold us accountable by simply having informed them. If you are the only one who knows, accountability can't exist.

38. **Inform everyone about the goal's importance.** Everyone needs to connect to the goals, but don't just tell, ask. Most of the time, the answers are sitting in the room with your team.

39. **Offer support.** When your colleagues are the owners, ask how you can support them or what responsibility you have to ensure their results.

40. **Apply accountability language with all stakeholders.** Initiate everyone in meaningful partnering and high-accountability conversations. Do others outside your immediate sphere drop the ball? Accountable relationships can extend to coworkers, customers, and vendors.

41. **Give others a chance.** You can spread opportunities to more people. Ownership for outcomes should only be given to experts about 80 percent of the time. If the choice jobs always go to your best people, no one else has an opportunity to learn and be prepared for promotions or other responsibilities when your experts are unable to work. Besides, if you overload your experts, they will burn out.

42. **Leaders at every level.** Accountability requires that leaders exist at every level and in every position. You can generate leadership at every level by treating others as if they are leaders—because they are, especially when you see them demonstrating the tips in this book.

43. **Tell stories.** You can probably remember an impactful story. Your organization is filled with stories

about how accountability paid off and when it didn't. Stories that have actually been experienced are the best. Identify situations when teams took risks or went above and beyond to ensure accountability that led to an exciting payoff. If you don't have your own story, borrow one from a colleague. For example, one of our clients helped a frustrated customer. Instead of saying, "Don't worry, I'll take care of this," our client said, "You will have the delivery in hand by 4 p.m. Pacific Time today."

44. **Offer first.** All eyes will be on you when you announce that you support accountability. People will be watching. You can model accountability by taking a leap of faith to always offer first—information, data, help, resources—whatever it takes to support others to be successful. Your actions will be noticed.

45. **Use the secret language.** Are you searching for the must-do to strengthen your organization's culture of accountability? Use the language of accountability throughout your area first. Then spread it throughout your organization. The language of accountability is the language of this book. We call it the secret language of high performance: clarity and specificity.

CHAPTER 4

USE MEETINGS TO GUIDE THE WAY

D o some of your meetings suck?

They don't have to. Meetings are a necessary part of every project and are often used to clarify and direct individual actions. As a reminder, all meetings should:

- Start and end on time;
- Be necessary, otherwise you should cancel if there is a better way to achieve the objective;
- Publish agendas in advance (with the most important items listed first);
- Use agendas that identify objectives, who's responsible, and time allowed;
- Restate action items at the end of each meeting;

- Only invite those who need to attend; and,
- Consider holding shorter, stand-up meetings whenever possible.

Meetings at a high-performing organization built on accountability go one step further. They emphasize what's needed to achieve goals and objectives.

When run well, meetings will be energizing, and you will look forward to the next one.

Tips to Use at Meetings for Accountability

46. **Anyone may add to the agenda.** Are you looking for a fast way to increase meeting involvement? If you allow those invited to add agenda items, they'll become more engaged and you'll promote ownership. Besides, they may see an element of the topic that wasn't apparent to you.

47. **Use a facilitator.** If you anticipate a controversial topic, or if your group tends to bog down, hire a facilitator who does not have a vested interest in the outcome. As a neutral party, the facilitator can manage the process, which frees you to be a part of the team discussion.

48. **Implement the "everyone speaks first" rule.** When you need to encourage ideas, you can use meetings to collect multiple perspectives before making decisions. To do this, implement an "everyone speaks first" rule. This means that no one speaks a second time about an issue until everyone has spoken once.

49. **Leaders speak last.** To prevent influencing others, leaders must voice their opinions last. This is especially valuable for a controversial decision when everyone has a unique perspective. Of course, during a

crisis, a leader makes fast decisions and announces them to spark immediate action.

50. **Ask more than you tell.** Are you looking for more ideas from others? Try asking more open-ended questions. For example, you might say, "Based on everything we've said, how do you see the path forward?" or "What do you see as our next steps?"

51. **Listen to the no's.** Do you have naysayers on your team? That could be good news. Listen intently to those who disagree with you. Be interested in the opinions of people who think differently than you do, as well as those who think like you do. The best ideas often come from the dissenters at your meeting.

52. **Invite strategically.** If you don't want to hear from a particular person, don't invite the individual to the meeting. It's that simple!

53. **Disinvite strategically.** If you have legacy team members who are no longer contributing, give them the gift of time by disinviting them.

54. **Reduce repeats.** Don't waste time by allowing someone to repeat something that has already been said. Note ideas on a flipchart page in full view—especially if the comments are for a future discussion. Enlist all meeting attendees to enforce "no repeats."

55. **Produce a positive path.** Have you ever been in a meeting that is stuck? You can take control of a meeting when there is too much focus on the past or the problem. Reverse the momentum by saying something like, "We've done a great job of defining the problem. How will we work together to solve it?"

56. **Paraphrase to understand.** Have you experienced a time when everyone left a meeting, but few knew what to do next? Ensure that roles, responsibilities, and the path forward are clear by encouraging all participants to paraphrase what they believe should happen next.

57. **Cancel when you can.** If you can't justify a meeting other than the fact that you've always had one, and if you don't think there is a good reason, you might want to try canceling. The best way to determine if a meeting is really needed is to cancel and see if anyone complains or if something doesn't get done.

58. **Evaluate the cost.** Calculate the cost of your meeting with a rough estimate of everyone's hourly pay to ensure you are getting an appropriate return on your investment.

59. **End with laser focus.** When you summarize the action items at the end of each meeting, you'll ensure

clear expectations. State who (owner) will do what (clear expectation) by when (stated date, time, and time zone) and with whom the action will be shared.

CHAPTER 5

REMAIN ON TRACK WITH ACCOUNTABLE FEEDBACK

One of Elaine's first supervisors gave feedback—lots of it. The only problem was that it was the same every time. "Nice job," he'd say in a guttural tone. Elaine ached to hear anything that would help her grow. Even, "That's crappy" (another word from his extensive vocabulary) would have been more helpful! At least she could have asked what needed to be done to make her performance less "crappy." To this day, Elaine grimaces when someone says, "Nice job," no matter the occasion.

Giving and receiving feedback—with others or in an accountability partnership—is an important part of achieving results. You probably know the basics of giving feedback: be honest and direct, state observed behaviors, time it close to the action, specify impact, and offer support when appropriate. Feedback helps everyone stay on track and improve.

Our 131 tips introduce the idea of using accountability partners. These partnerships can help you with both professional and personal commitments, such as losing weight, reducing time on Facebook, or repairing a relationship. Whether you request feedback from your accountability partner, or you receive it unrequested, you should welcome feedback with gratitude. It will make you a better person.

Accountable feedback requires you to go beyond feedback basics. These tips provide ideas on how feedback can benefit you.

Tips for Accountable Feedback

60. **Keep everyone informed.** When you are the owner, you have a responsibility to provide feedback about progress on your task. Keep it real: real-time (before you miss a deadline) and real-world (explain what challenges may exist).

61. **Invite feedback.** If you are not getting feedback, it doesn't necessarily mean you are doing a great job. You may not be hearing it because people have given up or don't feel safe giving you feedback. Ask others what they think you should start doing, stop doing, and do more often to be a better contributor.

62. **Feedback builds accountability.** What's the secret for receiving feedback—especially when it's negative? Respect who's offering it, listen actively, don't become defensive or argumentative, continue breathing (!), and ask yourself, "How can I grow from this?" If necessary, take time to think about the feedback and be willing to change your behavior. Feedback is a necessity in an environment of accountability to learn all information; you can't act on what you don't know. Don't become a feedback feuder!

63. **Be thankful.** Are you wondering how to respond to encourage feedback? First, thank people when they bring you feedback. Even if you disagree internally, there was something that led to their perception. Next, figure out what caused the perception and make an adjustment to prevent it in the future. Your "thank you" does double duty. First, it gives you information. Second, it builds trust so your feedback providers will continue to be open with you.

64. **Give feedback early and often.** Frequent and actionable feedback gives people a continuous perspective on how to be better, and it can head off bigger issues down the road. At the same time, make consequences and rewards clear. When possible, end your feedback session with an actionable tip.

65. **Expect the best of others.** An environment of accountability requires that you believe in other's potential. Do you have a mindset that ensures that giving feedback is positive? You can start today! Assume that everyone wants to, and has the ability to, improve. When you give up on someone, you also give up on potentially positive results.

66. **Make feedback specific.** Don't tell me I have "bad people skills." Tell me I "lack empathy when others

are telling me about sharing their troubles. As a result, they don't feel heard."

67. **Balance past and future.** How can you make feedback a part of the Accountability Method™ process? Try balance. While discussing a current project, balance giving constructive feedback on past performance with feed-forward for future opportunities. For example, "Up to this point, we've barely made our milestones. Perhaps if you move your review meetings earlier, we would have a little breathing room."

68. **Feedback isn't easy.** Nobody said it was easy! When feedback is difficult, you might ask for permission to share your comments. You could say something like, "I have an observation that I'd like to share. Can you suggest a good time to do that?" Contrasting statements can be a good lead in, such as, "Overall, I think we work well together, but lately I've noticed you interrupt me during our meetings." In other cases you may want to create vulnerability by saying, "I need to discuss something, but I am not sure how to approach it."

69. **Provide upstream feedback.** You think you're doing a great job but your boss isn't. We've heard that before! In a high-accountability culture, it is your

responsibility to communicate the truth upstream and in a way that it builds the relationship. Are you the boss? Start by making sure that everyone on your team is comfortable giving you feedback.

70. **Subtle feedback.** Are you sure that you are not communicating unintended feedback to others? For example, when you are the requester, consider who you choose to be project owners. Of course you want the most reliable owner, but it may appear that you are playing favorites. You know that when everyone does not have equal opportunity, it prevents others from developing new skills.

71. **Coach new team members.** What's the best thing you can do to welcome new members onto your team? Coach them on how to win with accountability. Use feedback to share how new people can be accountable members of your team. Share the tips in this book!

72. **Select an accountability partner.** What can you do to receive personal feedback to ensure your growth? Choose an accountability partner—someone who has your best interests at heart, who will be assertive and has the courage to tell you when you are incorrect, and someone who will challenge you when you are falling behind on your commitments. Of course,

you must be willing to be vulnerable to hear candid and honest feedback. Ideally the person will be an objective peer or someone outside your organization—definitely not your direct reports or your boss. They should care about your career and be assertive enough to tell you what you need to hear.

73. **Make feedback your friend.** To do so, alert those with whom you've shared your goal so they know specifically how often and in what communication format you would like to receive feedback. Include specific dates, times, and time zones when necessary.

74. **Offer to coach.** Does someone on your team need help? Reach out to a colleague who is struggling with a skill that you have expertise in and offer to coach them using what you know about giving constructive feedback.

75. **Personalize feedback.** Accountability works best when you realize that everyone is an individual and feedback needs to be personalized. All team members have their moments of excellence. By recognizing and rewarding this, you're reinforcing their accountability.

Chapter 6

Avoid Bad Directions and Potholes Along the Way

Seth, the new executive director, was seething!

The strategic plan was created during a two-day offsite at a modern, high-tech retreat center. Now it was time for the quarterly review and virtually nothing had been accomplished. What had gone wrong?!

As it turns out, lots had gone wrong. A nice meeting space was not enough. Tasks were assigned to regions, departments, and teams so no one person was accountable. Objectives were not clearly aligned to the organization's strategy. The team neglected to include timelines and milestones.

There had been no follow-up since the retreat. Previous strategic plans were put on the shelf, ignored and forgotten, so no one paid any attention to this one, either.

Problems will occur—of that you can be sure. Perhaps not to the extent as Seth's, but the potential for these pitfalls is why accountability must be approached with patience, integrity, and a vow to make it work over time.

Tips to Avoid Problems

76. **Reset expectations.** Are you introducing something new and different? Issue a fair warning if you change a standard or start to enforce an existing standard that has always been ignored. Reset everyone's expectations in advance. This is not about catching people doing something wrong. "I know we have talked about this in the past and haven't done it. I'm committed to it now, and I'm requesting that you join me. I believe we can do better."

77. **Clarify, clarify, clarify.** Don't understand? If you believe you're being tasked with a weak or ineffective project plan, ask the requester what outcome they are trying to achieve. Perhaps you can engineer a more effective and efficient plan to achieve the same outcomes. Ask for time to review the plan if you need it. Offer an exact time and place when you will get back to the requester.

78. **Tell 'em.** You may be asked to do something by someone who doesn't understand all that's required. It happens all the time. They may not know how much work is involved, and they may not know your other priorities, the approval process, how many stakeholders it touches, or what needs to be

put in place first. Inform them of the details involved for execution.

79. **Ask 'em.** Once you have laid out your understanding of the details to complete the project, ask people, "What have I missed?"

80. **Spread the word.** Inform all stakeholders when something will affect them. Sometimes you may inadvertently hear about a situation that affects others. Be a responsible team player and keep others in the know with communication. It doesn't matter if you are the newest hire or the CEO. If you are aware of information, tell everyone who may be impacted. Avoid wrong moves. Be accountable to quickly share what you know.

81. **Talk timeline, not deadline.** You probably know that clearly defining deadlines is good. Did you know that defining timelines is better? How can timelines help? It helps the receiver of the task to break the goal down into smaller, more manageable steps. It makes it easier to estimate how much time the full task will take. It also gives the requester an opportunity to offer constructive feedback along each step about small adjustments, as well as praise for what is working well.

82. **Frontload accountability.** Instead of focusing on what goes wrong when deadlines are missed, frontload accountability to define results before the task begins. Henry once encouraged a manufacturing company to review and plan their day in the morning. They insisted that they did not have time. Henry's response was, "But you have time to add a layer of inspection that results in redoing the work at the end of the day using twice the materials and labor at double the cost?" Don't let that happen to you. Frontload your tasks with specific and clear expectations and assignments.

83. **Own it.** Did you mess up? If you cause an error, offer no excuses or explanations. We cannot be perfect. All of us may fail to deliver what we promised. It's human nature. Simply state what you will do to repair the damage and avoid repeating it.

84. **Confronting is okay.** Were you taught to avoid confrontation? It depends on how you confront and why. Isolate the idea from the person and follow what we say in our book, *Step Up*: "Attack the idea, not the person." Respectfully confronting a peer when there is an issue builds trust, solves problems faster, and opens doors to creativity and innovation. Don't believe it? Try it.

85. **Monitor progress.** The highest-performing people are usually intrinsically self-motivated; but this isn't true for everyone. Remember that it's important to establish timelines with specific, short-term, measurable results along the way. When someone is watching us, we usually perform to our best abilities. If you develop a timeline with others and share progress and improvements required as you go, they are more likely to excel. Monitoring each other's progress motivates everyone to be more productive and accountable.

86. **Never pad a due date.** If you deal with someone who is constantly late, your first thought may be to request a due date earlier than necessary. ***Don't do it.*** In the spirit of true transparency, honesty, and openness, this would be a lie. Instead, schedule mid-checks and milestones. Padding due dates is bad business. You will gain a reputation for asking for things earlier than you really need them.

87. **Pre-negotiate. Introduce a new word to your team.** "Pre-negotiate" means that individuals do not wait until they miss a deadline. Instead, the owner informs everyone who needs to know as soon as a delay is anticipated. The timing for a pre-negotiated review occurs before the due date and retains the

owner's credibility. Everyone on your team wins with this one.

88. **Identify good pairings.** Are you looking for development opportunities? Pair team members who are positive about accountability with individuals who may not see the value in an accountable culture. More positive members are great role models for those who tend to lean toward negativity.

89. **Invite your pessimists to the party.** If you work with people who seem to be negative, try these questions to turn them around: What challenge do you see? What suggestions do you have to avoid your concern? How can you positively influence the challenge our team is facing? They may see roadblocks and challenges that you do not.

90. **Visit unreliability.** You'll drive accountability by investing in the right people, but you still need to give others a chance. When asking for a commitment from those who have a less-than-stellar record of meeting commitments, you'll have more success if you visit them in person and look them in the eye. Emails and texts are less reliable forms of communication. A personal visit with a verbal commitment will be more successful.

91. **Ask why, not who.** Sometimes, no matter what you do, things happen that are outside of everyone's control. When that happens, figure out why, learn from it, and determine what you can do to prevent it from happening again. Find out why something occurred—not who was responsible.

92. **Conduct a post-mortem review.** What went well? What didn't? What will we do differently next time? Some organizations do this after every large project, whether it was successful or not, to obtain lessons learned so they can improve the process.

93. **Avoid wrong turns with a pre-mortem.** In his book, *When: The Scientific Secrets of Perfect Timing*, author Daniel Pink introduces the concept of a pre-mortem. As you might guess, a pre-mortem is conducted before you embark on a project. Pink suggests that you ask, "Imagine that it is 12 months and this project is a disaster. What went wrong?" Your team will anticipate and avoid potential mistakes.

94. **Focus, don't wander.** New problems will crop up. When they do, you'll need to make a rational decision about where you'll spend your time. It is easy to get sidetracked from priorities. You want to be flexible, of course, but taking on a new problem

should be a choice, not a diversion. Don't stray; stay on your priority path.

95. **Uncover your Glossary of Failure™.** Having delivered accountability content in more than 80 countries, we know that all ages, genders, and countries have a Glossary of Failure™—unclear language like "ASAP" or "soon"—that is alive and well. We all get lazy and use common words and phrases that do not have the same meaning for everyone, such as ASAP, try, end of the day/week/ month, soon, or right away. Make a list of your Glossary of Failure™ terms and identify substitutes that meet the language of accountability rigor.

96. **Check yourself before you wreck yourself.** Wonder how you're doing? Conduct an audit on your most recent emails and texts. Have you been communicating with words from your Glossary of Failure™? If so, stop and replace those terms with specifics.

97. **Clarify requests.** Remember to clarify others' ambiguous requests with the language of specificity such as, "What time and date shall I follow up with you to close the loop?" or "Can you describe the final result for which you're asking my commitment?"

98. **Eliminate ambiguity.** Errors occur when specificity of language is missing. Remove all ambiguity so that everyone can measure outcomes in specific terms, including timelines and metrics. Ambiguity kills accountability.

99. **Value differences.** You'll thrive when you can see the value of individual differences and can learn to tolerate mistakes. If necessary, seek non-punitive strategies to challenge destructive behavior, such as: coaching for improved performance; redirecting negative conversations; affirming concerns followed by an action plan; or even simply listening.

100. **Build trust.** Low trust equals high fear. The best way to build trust is to be vulnerable by admitting when you have made a mistake and/or don't know something.

CHAPTER 7

ENSURE YOUR TEAM IS HEADING TO THE SAME DESTINATION

Jannha ran down the hall, bumping headlong into Carlos. He grabbed her armful of folders just as they exploded in midair. "Whoa!" he said, "What's the rush?" Breathlessly, Jannha said, "I've a tight deadline before our meeting this afternoon, and I forgot to send reminders. I just learned that Josie is ill and can't contribute her section." Carlos responded, "I'm on it. And by the way, the email I just sent can wait until next week. How else can I help?"

An accountable culture requires positive team relationships.

Emotional Safety® is an element of building positive team relationships where everyone feels safe and appreciated. This was obvious in Carlos and Jannha's relationship. When Emotional Safety® becomes a part of the culture of accountability, everyone is encouraged to speak up, to deliver bad news as well as good, and to be honest and vulnerable. Emotional Safety® means being comfortable with uncomfortable discussions—those that create emotional responses. When teams feel safe challenging each other, they deliver more innovation, better decisions, and better results.

The big payoff for building positive team relationships is high performance, higher than your competitors.

Tips to Build Team Relationships

101. **Build teams.** If your team has formed recently or has faced obstacles, it may require an opportunity to gain or regain its identify to increase accountability. A team-building event away from the office affords team members time to explore concerns and have an opportunity to improve individual and team relationships. This may be just what they need to define and agree on accountability behaviors.

102. **Offer help.** When you know someone has a critical commitment, demonstrate team accountability by offering support in any way you can. Ask yourself, "What can I do or stop doing that will be helpful?" For example, if you know that someone is on a tight deadline, you could hold off asking for information about something that is less time-sensitive.

103. **Remind gently.** Team members can hold each other accountable for personal changes. For example, if you know that someone wants to improve meeting management by restating actions at the end of a meeting, you can gently remind the meeting leader near the end by saying, "How about we save the last five minutes of this meeting to restate actions?"

104. **Take a timeout.** Have you ever had one of *those* days? We all have. Maintain team relationships by knowing yourself. For example, if you are too emotionally charged to continue a difficult discussion, request time. You could say, "I am feeling frustrated and am probably not objective right now. Can we discuss this tomorrow at 9 a.m. Eastern Time?"

105. **Person or the plan.** Participation from everyone is expected in an environment of accountability. However, there may be times when a colleague presents a plan or idea that you oppose—perhaps even strongly. Don't let your exasperation with the plan turn into irritation with the person. Attack the plan, not the person, with a comment such as, "I usually agree with your plans. Tell me why this makes sense for our team."

106. **Personalize interactions.** Before you choose efficiency over relationships, plan to make interactions as personal as possible. Create space for others to balance their own physical, mental, and spiritual energy with yours. When you need to communicate with people, maintain the best relationships by communicating in this order when possible: in-person; video conference; telephone; email or text.

107. **Reward the team.** Think about rewards that might inspire team members to exceed their goals. Self-esteem is boosted and rewarding results are produced when people reach their highest potential.

108. **Name the channel.** You can ask your team which communication channels they prefer for each type of communication, e.g., phone call or personal visit for changes, Outlook for meeting invitations, or Slack for project updates and questions.

109. **Accommodate time.** Be a time titan for those who need time with you. Make time and date commitments easy for the other person. For example, Asia Pacific colleagues often participate in meetings at night to accommodate Western business partners who work during the day. Consider times for those who work other shifts, too. And, when possible, give the boss a chance to be accommodating.

110. **Spotlight others.** You can build relationships by giving credit to others when defining a process or how to do something. For example, you could say, "When placing your ladder on an uneven surface, follow Andre's method to maintain safety."

111. **Create Emotional Safety.®** You can create an emotionally safe environment so everyone can be honest. This also frees them to be vulnerable, which is a

precursor to building trust and strong relationships. Want to double your investment? When people feel safe to share, you are more informed when making decisions.

112. **Engage with others.** You can build relationships by getting to know your team members personally. Make time to build a relationship that is both professional and personal. Learn to respect different cultures, norms, and expectations. Be aware of what works for others. Building relationships points the way to accountability.

113. **Meet together; eat together.** Reward success with your own forms of celebration. For example: Have managers cook and serve at a cookout; schedule monthly donuts and coffee with your workgroup to share the latest happenings; have a pizza lunch to say "thank you"—be sure to include virtual team members by sending them a pizza to share at the same time.

114. **Know what you project.** We judge ourselves by our intentions and what's on the inside. Others judge what they see on the outside. People deal with you based on what they see, not on what you think they should see. You are accountable for how you are

perceived. Learn how others perceive you and adjust your behaviors to project a more positive you.

115. **Don't be the "heroic" leader.** It's easy to understand how to support and help others when they need it. But be careful that you don't jump in to "save" your team with the right answer every time. At times, the team may need to be challenged to do better. Accountability ensures that individuals are learning and developing, but it's impossible to grow when someone is solving all their problems. Rushing in to the rescue is not always helpful. Solving problems can be a great learning experience, so let your people be the "hero" sometimes. Balance is key.

116. **Make it safe for people to be honest.** Make the first move to build trust. That may mean becoming vulnerable, which could seem risky. This is where Emotional Safety® works well. Opening up can help build trusting relationships. Vulnerability leads to trust; trust is the foundation for building strong relationships; and strong relationships are the cornerstone for high performance.

117. **Earn trust.** Trust isn't an entitlement. If you want to demonstrate trustworthiness, but don't know where to begin, try these for starters: Be yourself.

Do what you say you will do. Don't break confidences. Be honest and candid. Demonstrate competence and confidence. Relationships are almost always more important than any incident or disagreement.

CHAPTER 8

STAY ON THE ROAD TO CONTINUOUS SELF-IM-PROVEMENT

Accountability starts and ends with you. Your environment is constantly changing, so you need to learn, change, and grow to keep up. Don't get derailed from your learning journey.

There is always room for improvement for all of us, so what do we need to improve most (or first)? Communication? Technical expertise?

Clarity and specificity? Relationships? Meeting management? Delivering feedback? Which area of development will give you the fastest and/or most impactful ROI? So much to learn; so little time!

Self-improvement happens when you decide what to do and act on it. Keep your eyes on your goal, pay attention to how your development impacts others, and deal with obstacles along the way. Make a commitment to your ongoing personal learning. You know the drill by now: What will you do, by when, and who will you share it with?

Tips to Improve Yourself

118. **Take ownership of you.** As much as you may want to change others, you can only change yourself. You need to start with you. Focus the change on what you are responsible for and/ or have control or influence over. Ensure that you understand your role, goals, and responsibilities.

119. **Practice a learner's mindset.** You can clear your mind of preconceived ideas by preparing yourself to consider new information. Practice a *learner's mindset* and allow yourself to reconsider what you currently know. Make room to understand something new. Combine everything you learn then coach others to reach the same level of understanding.

120. **Never rest; personal best.** You want to be your best, right? Determine what you can invest in yourself based on the time and resources available to you. Make a list and discuss your plan with your supervisor or your accountability partner. Look for opportunities on your calendar to demonstrate new behaviors.

121. **Reflect on your results.** Personal change requires self-reflection. Make time to reflect on your

commitments and how you lived up to doing what you said you would do. Ask for input from others.

122. **What's blocking you?** Identify barriers that you think prevent you from accomplishing a goal. Eliminate thoughts like, "I'm too busy to learn" or "I have nothing new to learn." Create a plan that will give you a better chance to achieve your goal.

123. **Deal with reactions.** Here's a word of caution. Don't ignore the impact of your changes and how others may respond. They may inadvertently stifle your efforts. Tell others why you are pursuing your goals. Help them see how they can benefit from the changes you are making. Finally, enlist allies and gather a support network.

124. **Know your triggers.** We all have particular words that trigger a negative emotional response when someone says them. Think of your trigger words as a way people can push your buttons—even though they are probably unaware they upset you. Change how you react to these triggers. Identify your triggers and be honest about why they set you off. You can change your reaction to them.

125. **Plan it yourself; do it with an accountability partner.** You may think about doing or reading something to develop new skills or abilities. But it's easy

to let your intentions be overcome by other events. Instead, make a commitment to yourself to take action. Block time on your calendar. Treat that scheduled time as if it were a meeting with another person. Show up on time and focus on your planned event, whether it is reading a journal or practicing a new skill. Be accountable to yourself. For real accountability, enroll an accountability partner.

126. **Hear what you say.** Yes, we've all been communicating since we were born. With all that practice, we all ought to be perfect, right? No way! We all have room to improve our communication. It is not about what you say. Communication is how others interpret what they hear you say. Check it out by asking, "How do you interpret what I said?"

127. **Get a coach.** Seek to understand yourself better. A coach will listen, empathize, and encourage you to grow. We recommend that you partner with a business coach. A coach will help you see what you don't see and explore what you didn't even know was there. A coach is a good investment in your development.

128. **Assess yourself.** If you want to improve your skills and abilities, survey your team. To ensure complete candor, check with your human resources

department. They may direct you to a third-party vendor (like us), who can supply a 360-degree feedback instrument or our 180-degree approach: The Leadership Edge.™ Once you receive your survey results, meet with your coach or mentor to discuss what you can do to improve.

129. **Prioritize.** You don't have unlimited energy and time. Setting laser-sharp priorities is good for defining a clear path for business, and it's equally important for you.

130. **Stop doing.** Yep, this is going to take time. Perhaps one of the most useful things you can do is to create a "stop doing" list. Make a list of all the habits, routines, activities, or even people in your life that use your time but do not move you closer to your goals. Perhaps some of these activities are actually moving you further away from your desired priorities. Think of it as cleaning house for a better future.

131. **Accountability is about you.** It's all about you. Apply your energy to changing your own behavior—not changing others. Use the mirror/glass model from the Jim Collins classic, *Good to Great.* When you stand at a window and look out, it's easy to see what others are doing wrong; you'll waste energy deciding what they should be doing better. Instead,

give yourself more constructive feedback by looking into a mirror.

When you look in a mirror, you see only yourself. Use your energy to decide what you are doing well and what you could do better. Take the mirror/ glass test yourself. When things go well, look out the window and praise those who accomplished the feat. When things are not as successful, look in the mirror to determine what you could have done differently.

A FINAL THOUGHT ... OR 10!

Put your oxygen mask on first before helping others...

Accountability is about working hard, and it is also about knowing when to rest. Competitive athletes know that part of a winning training regimen is rest. Resting your mind, body, and spirit when you aren't competing helps you be more successful when you are. When you work, work hard; when you rest, rest hard. By resisting the urge to keep your mind busy, you will deliver a calm, clear-headed, mindful "self," make better decisions, and have a better ear for accountable language. This gives you and your team a competitive advantage.

As you move toward mastering accountability:

- You will offer realistic promises and hit your deadlines;
- You will be clear about your priorities, scheduling your time accordingly;
- You will value the people you work with—they can feel it, and they feel the same about you;
- Your meetings will be more productive; and,
- You will lead the organizational change— where your enthusiasm is contagious, no matter where you sit on the org chart.

There is no doubt, you are playing to win! Remember, this is an intellectually simple and behaviorally complex set of concepts. It takes time to create these new habits. Understanding them won't make you good at application; only practice will.

Here are our top 10 thoughts:

1. **Little things matter.** Accountability is a big topic. It's the small, minute-to-minute choices that make you an accountability master.
2. **Go first.** No matter what your position, or where you fall on the org chart, you can lead with accountability. Show others the way by modeling what you have learned.
3. **Disrupt normal.** The status quo has its place in the world, but not when you are trying to

create a competitive advantage. Be willing to disrupt what is normal with your new language.

4. **Keep it real.** Be authentic about how you feel. At the same time, be mindful of how you express yourself so that you can build relationships.

5. **Be vulnerable.** Trust is the foundation to all relationships; vulnerability is the conduit to trust. Commit to "owning" your mistakes openly, and your relationships will grow.

6. **Me first.** (Ah, but wait—not what you are thinking.) View accountability through an introspective lens. When facing an undesired outcome, look for your own contribution before blaming others.

7. **Develop yourself.** It is vital that you look for opportunities to be better. Disrupt your own normal and keep your learner's mindset.

8. **Listen without defending; speak without offending.** When receiving constructive input, replace your judgment with curiosity. Make it your job to understand why others feel the way they do.

9. **Express appreciation.** Thank people, be aware of when others are demonstrating excellence,

and acknowledge them—privately and publicly. Be specific. Do it often.

10. **Revisit this book.** Use this book as a best-practices field guide. Mark it up, add your own notes in the margins, and make it work for you. Share tips with your team. If you have a great tip, let us know at moreinfo@ dynamicresults.com. Your suggestion may make one of our monthly blogs. Our clients are our greatest assets. Many of these ideas come from clients, and we love to hear from you!

Please join us in the belief that you can effect change in your organization. You have the power to lead the way for others through the way you make accountable commitments and requests. Do this in a way that generates freedom for others, and they will see you as a champion in the organization. Be a model of accountability and you will drive it into your culture.

Five additional ways to create a high-accountability culture in your organization

1. **Take our free accountability challenge** at www.dynamicresults.com.

2. **Enroll in our Winning with Accountability™ eSchool,** which has been delivered in more than 80 countries with an average ROI of $16,000 per learner. This interactive eSchool teaches the entire Accountability Method™ in a way that creates sustainable performance improvement. It won the 2018 Brandon Hall Award for "Excellence in Learning."

3. **Check out our website** for additional information through blogs and videos at www.dynamicresults.com. Enroll in our Emotional Safety® eSchool.

4. **Invite Henry to keynote your next leadership conference.** Bring Henry Evans or one of our certified accountability masters to your organization for an interactive workshop. Contact us at 214-742-1403.

5. **Reinforce accountability** with cards, countdown timers, posters, and other books, such as the best-selling *Winning with Accountability* and the Amazon Top 10 best-seller *Step Up: Lead in Six Moments that Matter.*

ADDITIONAL RESOURCES

For a more in-depth look at *131 Ways to Win with Accountability* topics, read these blogs at www.dynamicresults.com:

- Three Rules for Choosing Accountability Partners
- Mastering Empathy in 3 Easy Steps
- Reversing the Polarity of Communications for Better Business Results
- Eradicate Excuses™ at Work in Three Easy Steps
- Driving Results—Accountability as a Competitive Advantage™
- Director of Emotional Safety®

ABOUT THE AUTHORS

Henry J. Evans is an invited agitator and chief peacemaker to the C-Suite, co-author of the Amazon Top 10 *Step Up: Lead in Six Moments that Matter*, and author of the best-selling *Winning with Accountability*. He keynotes globally on accountability and Emotional Safety.®

As co-founder and CEO (Change Excellence Officer) of Dynamic Results, he has delivered more than 10,000 hours of executive coaching and 3,000 hours of strategic planning sessions. Leveraging learning from numerous successes (and a failure) in his own career, with the wisdom of his clients, he helps them achieve better results.

Henry's concepts are published by Forbes, Inc., Fast Company, Entrepreneur, the BBC, and many other outlets. An award-winning instructor of MBA programs, his life mission is to "leave every person and situation better than I found them." Henry smashes myths about leadership, and he can be reached at hevans@dynamicresults.com.

Elaine Biech is a consultant, trainer, and author of *The Washington Post* No. 1 best-seller *The Art and Science of Training*. With more than three decades of experience and 80-plus published books, she has been called "the Stephen King of the training industry." She is a dedicated lifelong learner who believes that excellence isn't optional.

She delights in helping leaders maximize their effectiveness and guiding organizations to address large-scale change. The recipient of numerous professional awards, Elaine is a consummate training professional who has been instrumental in guiding the talent-development profession for most of her career.

Thank you for reading

131 Ways to Win with Accountability!

We hope it has assisted you in your quest for personal and professional growth.

CornerStone Leadership's mission is to fuel knowledge with practical resources that will accelerate

your success and life satisfaction!

www.CornerStoneLeadership.com